HOW TO FIN

YOUR
LOVE
GURU

For A Lifetime of Happiness

Rachel Jones

Table of Contents

PART 1

Chapter 1:
6 Ways To Flirt With Someone

No matter how confident and bold we assume ourselves to be, we tend to freeze up and utter a wimpy 'hey' when we see our crush approaching us. Flirting doesn't always come easily to everyone, and there's always struggle, awkwardness, and shyness that follows. But, some people are natural-born flirters and just get the dating thing right.

Knowing how to flirt and actually showing someone that you're interested in them sexually or romantically can be a minefield. But once you get your hands on it, you'll probably become an expert in no time. If you struggle with flirting, we've got some tips to help you master the art of flirting and getting your crush's attention. Below are some ways to flirt with someone successfully.

Be Confident But Mysterious

There's nothing sexier than someone who has a lot of confidence. Of course, I'm not talking about being too overconfident, and it will tend to push people away from you. But if you're strutting down the halls as you own them, your crush (and everyone else) will notice you. Don't give away too much of yourself while being confident. People tend to get intrigued by someone who gives off mysterious vibes. They show their interest in you and avail every opportunity to try to get to know you better. This will lead to you having a chance to make up a good conversation with your crush and even flirt with them in between.

Show That You're Interested In Their Life

Who doesn't love compliments and talking about themselves all the time? We come along with people who mostly like to talk than to listen. If you get a chance to talk to your crush, don't waste it. Ask them questions about their life, get to know their views and ideas about certain things like politics, fashion, controversies, show that you're genuinely interested in them. They will love your curious nature and would definitely look forward to having another conversation with you. This will also give your brownie points of getting to know them better.

Greet Them Whenever You Pass Them

Seeing your crush approach you or simply seeing them standing in the halls can be the scariest feeling ever. You will probably follow your gut reaction and become nervous; either you'll walk past them hurriedly or look down at your phone and pretend like you're in the middle of a text conversation battle. But you have to ignore those instincts, and you have to look up at them and simply smile. You don't have to indulge yourself in an extensive conversation with them. Just taking a second to wave or say hi can be more than enough to get yourself on your crush's radar, as you will come off as polite to them.

Make Ever-So-Slight Contact

The sexiest touches are often those electric ones that come unexpectedly, not the intentional ones that might make someone uncomfortable. Unnecessary touches can be a turn-on because they signal a willingness to venture beyond the safe boundaries that we usually maintain between ourselves and others. But be careful not to barge into them accidentally. Small, barely-there touches that only the two of you notice are the best. Let your foot slightly touch theirs or lightly brush past them.

Compliment Them

While everyone loves receiving compliments, try not to go overboard, or they would be more likely to squirm in their seat rather than ask you out. You should compliment them lightly about their outfit or fragrance or their features or personality, but keep the subtle flirtation for when the time and moment is right. Giving them compliments would make them think that you're interested in them and want to step up the equation with them.

Look At Them

Experts suggest that we look and then look away three times to get someone's attention. According to the Social Issues Research Centre, maintaining too much eye contact while flirting is people's most common mistake. Our eyes make a zigzag motion when we meet someone new - we look at them from eye to eye and then the nose. With friends, we look below their eye level to include the nose and mouth. The subtle flirt then widens that triangle to incorporate parts of the body. Please don't stare at someone too intensely, or else you'll end up making them feel uncomfortable.

Conclusion

It might seem nerve-wracking to put yourself out there and start flirting, but fear not! It's normal to get nervous around someone whom you like. Follow the above ways to seem confident and pull off a successful flirtation. Know the importance of keeping a balance between revealing your feelings and keeping the person you like intrigued.

Chapter 2:

9 Signs an Introvert Likes You

A lot of people out there are conscious to know about the tell-tale signs that reveal if an Introvert Likes You or not. You are probably unsure if someone you know has a secret crush on you and you are eager to find out so that you can reciprocate those feelings, or maybe you want to be find out - out of mere curiosity.

Well, I want to first say that because there are many different kinds of introverts, we may not be able to cover all aspects of it. Some introverts like to be alone in their own comfort zones while others like to hang out with their inner circle of close friends and relatives. But basically an introvert is generally shy and more reserved by nature. They are usually more quiet and may seem like they have built up a little wall around them in the initial meetings you have with them.

In today's video, we are going into 9 specific signs than an Introvert Likes You. Hopefully this will shed a brighter light on this topic and bring you some lightbulb moments. So without any further delay, let's get right into it.

Number one

They will Try to Open up

Introverts are shy creatures that look for soul connection like a meeting of minds. So when an introvert likes you, they will try to open up, they will try to share their thoughts and feelings with you. They will tell you about that one best day of their life and they will tell you how they feel about themselves asking you, do you feel the same way?

So if an introvert overshares with you then you can take it as a plus point as they don't tell these things just to anyone. They tell you these things because you are special to them and they want you to share your world of thoughts too.

Number two

They Know A Lot About You

You might be amazed at this one and might be thinking, how can an introvert know that much about me so quickly? Ahmm, never underestimate their researching skills, just saying. If an introvert likes you then they could potentially look you up on social media, they might check out your posts to get to know who you are as a person a little more. They do their own behind-the-scenes search because they may be too shy to ask you in person, or they might do so to feel that they feel like they may know more about you before committing to liking you. So if they know these little details about you then there is a high chance that they do indeed like you.

Number three

They Will Be First To View Or Like Whatever You Post On Social Media

This one also comes under the previous point. If an introvert likes you, they might be the first to like your post on social media because they may be too shy to message you directly or tell you in person that they find you interesting. An introvert will leave breadcrumbs behind to show that they are interested in you. So yeah, you gotta check if they are doing it or not.

Number four

They Look At You More Than Usual People

If an introvert likes you then they will surely check you out. Whenever they come in front of you or if you are sitting in a group then that introvert will look at you like more than once, without making you feel uncomfortable. Yes! They have this talent. So if you catch them looking at you, then they are probably into you.

Number five

Laughing Nervously

If an Introvert likes you then they might shutter or blush in your presence as well as laugh nervously. They can also get tongue-tied while talking to you. Want to know the reason? Let me tell you. When an introvert talks to you, they are actually out of their comfort zone, so that's why they appear hyper-alert. They are putting themselves out there. Give them the space to be themselves if they appear to be acting this way.

Number six

Immediately Answer your Call Or They Call You

Introverts generally don't like taking calls. It would not be wrong to say that they let all calls go to the voicemail unless it's the call from their food delivery guy. So if an introvert picks up your calls or calls you to talk to you then they might be head over heels over you.

Number seven

Inviting You To Hangouts

Here, I would go back to the first point where I said, introverts don't share their private world with a normal person. Introverts don't go out much but still, they have some favorite places like a coffee shop, a park that makes them feel good, or a hiking trail. So if an introvert takes you to these kinds of places, it means they want to share some part of what makes them feel good.

Number eight

They Step Out Of Their Comfort Zone

This is the most that an introvert can do for you. Do you imagine how difficult it is to step out of your comfort zone? Not everyone can do it except for the person who likes you unconditionally. So if an Introvert likes you, they would love to go to parties, or in a music festival only if they know you would be there. They can stay up late at night just to talk to you and to spend some time with you.

Number nine

Writing "Love Messages"

Now, you might be thinking if a person writes us a love letter then it's an obvious thing that they like us, how is it a sign then? Let me tell you how. Actually, an introvert's love message is different from others.

They write things like, hey, how are you? How's your day going? Now, these things are common for an extrovert, they can ask these things to anyone but for an introvert, these messages are like love letters. As you know, introverts don't like talking much face to face so they explain their feelings by writing you a letter or sending you a text.

And writing is the apple pie of introverts. In writing, they can explain how they feel about you without being deficient of words but they will not do it. Introverts!! So if you are getting this kind of message or letters from an introvert, then it's an obvious thing that they like you.

So that's it, guys, we are done with our today's topic of nine Signs an Introvert Likes You. Now, it's time for you to share your thoughts. What do you think about these signs? Have you got your answer yet or not? And if you are an introvert then let us know if there are some additional things to help others. If you got value from this video then smash the like button and don't forget to subscribe to our channel as we will be talking about some amazing topics in the future. See you soon!

Chapter 3:

6 Dating Red Flags To Avoid

When dating someone, there always stands a risk. A risk of not being happy or a threat of choosing the wrong person. That is why elders taught us to make smart decisions smartly. But what can one do when it comes to finding the one. Acknowledging a person you want to date won't be enough. Many factors revolve around dating. That is why it is essential to recognize red flags in your relationship. So, we should never hurry to commit to someone. Take your time. There is a lot more than getting to know this person. When initially dating, we always need to make sure to know where our comfort zone lies.

Red flags are the danger signs of a relationship. It can save you a lot of time and positivity. And it's not necessarily true that only the other person is to blame. Sometimes we fail to give them our part of affection, and gradually it becomes a disaster. Even if we overlook the minor toxicity, ignoring the major red flags is not suitable for you. Don't hesitate to give your opinion.

1. Shortfall Of Trust

The one major thing we all need to date someone is trust. Doubt will only make things difficult for you and your partner. Trusting each other is vital in a relationship. And when you date someone, trust grows slowly. And if your growth is based on lies and cheating, then that trust is as thin as thread. You can't force yourself to trust them either. If it doesn't come naturally, count it as a significant red flag because trust is the first thing that comes when dating someone.

2. Change In Personality

In a relationship, we have often seen people change their personalities around different people. If the same is happening to you, then you have to be careful. If they act differently around you, it indicates that they are not themselves in front of you. That is one major red flag in dating that shouldn't be ignored. They try to act the way you would like, instead of the course you are in. And eventually, they will get frustrated. So, it's better to be yourself around everyone. That way, your relationship will be genuine, and you feel a lot happier.

3. Toxicity

An abusive relationship is the worst kind. When someone is not attentive towards you or shouts at you constantly, you become the submissive one. It would be best if you took a stand for yourself equally. Most of the time, people stay quiet in times like these. But it's to be known that it is a dangerous sign in your dating life. It's a red flag that needs to be taken into notice. You don't have to cope with them; leave them be. Find someone who matches your energy. A toxic person is just as bad as drugs. We need to be careful around them.

4. Feeling Insecure

Sometimes, a relationship that is not meant to be, leaves you feeling insecure about yourself. You constantly question your place in that relationship. Where do you stand in their life? It leaves you thinking about all the flaws you have and examining all the wrong decisions. You have to know that it works both ways. And whoever they are, they have to accept you no matter what. You start to contribute more than your partner when it should be all about equality.

5. Not Being Around Each Other

When we dive into a relationship, we feel the need to be comforted. And when the person opposite you makes you feel uncomfortable, it's a major red flag in your dating life. You both need to make sure to be there for support. If not, then that relationship doesn't hold any significant meaning. If we do not feel secure or satisfied, then what do we get from this relationship? Because that is the most important thing that we might need from someone. But it's essential to play your part as well. Both sides should give their all for their dating to work.

6. Keeps Secrest From You

What someone needs in a relationship is to share their lives. Talking is the basis of communication that builds a relationship. But if your partner keeps secrets, then how can you grow together? You always need to speak for better understanding and comfort with each other. If they are acting fishy, you can't spy on them. It's a red flag that you need to catch.

Conclusion

You need someone who provides you with what you deserve. If you feel someone is not suitable for you, then feel free to break up with them. It would help if you were your priority. And make sure others know how important you are to yourself and should be important to them too.

Chapter 4:

7 Ways To Make A Girl Like You

You might have always wondered, "what does that popular guy do that makes all the girls hover around him like bees," or, instead, you may think that girls are too picky and hard to impress, not your cup of tea at all! There's absolutely nothing you can do that will make a woman like you instantly, but if you vow to remain patient and follow these tips that I am about to give you, you may get the girl you've always wanted.

Here are 7 ways to make a girl like you:

1. Looks aren't everything

It's true that getting girls to like you can seem complicated and confusing. Getting their attention is no piece of cake either. And God forbid if you say or do the wrong thing at the wrong time, you can lose her interest in a heartbeat. A lot of the guys assume that looks are the only thing that matters to a woman. Well, that's somewhat wrong. For most women, a man's personality traits (e.g., his confidence, his charm, his masculinity, his gentle and caring nature, and most importantly, his sense of humor) carry much more weight than looks. If the guy is average-looking with a 10/10 personality, he would be considered as appealing and attractive by the woman.

2. Don't pretend to be 'just friends with her.

The most common mistake that men make is that they approach the girl intending to be their friends first. They think that being all friendly and pleasant to her, listening to all her problems, gossiping with her, and always being there for her will eventually trigger the feelings inside her. She would magically start to like him. They don't know that once the girl starts seeing you as her friend only, then there's no other option for her to consider regarding you. You shouldn't cross the line, but you should make her feel interested in you by flirting with her, giving her clues, and making small gestures like giving her flowers and asking her out on lunch or dinner. You should be able to spark up the feelings inside her or wait till someone else does, and you'll be left listening to how amazing the other guy is.

3. Don't Tell Her You Like Her Unless You're Sure That She Does Too

If you haven't ignited her feelings for you or made much of an effort that showed that you're attracted to her and suddenly tells her out of the blue that you like her, then boy, do I have bad news for you. This would make the girl lose interest in you completely. While it's true that you should always be honest about your feelings, it should also be considered that sometimes you have to let the other person act and see if they feel the same about you. You should make her feel special and loved without expressing yourself first. Eventually, she'll start to warm up to you. And when she is drooling all over you with your fantastic personality traits and be attracted to you, that's when it's time to let your emotions out.

4. Be patient if she tests you.

A girl will definitely try to test whether the guy can be considered for the long run or not. If she approaches you with a stern look and acts unfriendly, or if she's teasing you with playful banter, she's trying to test your confidence and see how you'll react in different situations. A guy who understands this will remain confident and relaxed and may even counterattack the girl, which will eventually make the girl more interested in him. On the other hand, an insecure guy will take this change in behaviour as a sign of rejection and may feel left out. A woman always needs a man who is confident enough to take whatever she throws at him. A charming and assertive personality is a significant turn-on for women.

5. Make her laugh.

A good sense of humour is the one trait girls will die upon. Many studies suggest that being attracted to a person with a good sense of humour has a much higher ratio than those with little to no sense of humour. If a girl is romantically interested in you at a subconscious level, her eyes will dart at you first when she laughs. But don't try too hard; you don't want to come off as a clown or a stand-up comedian. Just go with the flow; the off-the-cuff humour can also be considered helpful.

6. Talk about your mutual interests.

Ask her about her hobbies, passions, phobias, favourite music, favourite artist, favourite movies/tv shows, and maybe you might be surprised that you, too, share the mutual taste in these things. Tell her all about yours too; maybe your favourite movie is hers too. Or perhaps the song that makes you cry makes her whimper too. And if not, start showing interest in her stuff. Watch her favourite TV show, listen to her favourite music. Suggest her some of your own. And then bond with her over them.

7. Shower her with compliments and meaningful gestures.

Compliment her now and then, but don't go too overboard. Drooling over her can have the completely opposite effect. Notice her outfit and tell her how amazing the colour looks on her, or compliment how beautiful her smile is. Send her cute little letters or texts that would remind her of you or suggest that she crossed your mind. Send her flowers randomly that will make her day. Plan something special just for the both of you. Put efforts to make her feel that she holds some importance in your life. Keep it sweet and simple.

Conclusion:

Getting a girl to like you is more accessible than most of the guys think. When you'll display your traits and characteristics and be honest and authentic to her, she will instinctively like you and feel drawn and attracted towards you. Making a girl feel special and happy is not a challenging task at all. It only requires a little effort and small unique gestures that will make them like you in no time.

Chapter 5:

6 Signs Your Love Is One-Sided

While some things are better one-sided, like your favorite ice-cream cone that you don't want to share, your high school diary that knows all your enemies and crushes, and a game of solitaire. But a healthy relationship? Now that should be a two-sided situation. Unfortunately, when you're stuck in a one-sided relationship, it becomes easy to fool yourself every day that what you are experiencing is normal, when in reality, it could actually be toxic or even unworthy and loveless.

They could physically be sitting next to you, but you will find yourself being alone because of your emotional needs not being taken care of. Even though you have committed yourself to your partner, there's a fundamental difference between being selfless in love and giving it all without receiving anything at all. It might be possible that you're in denial, but the below signs of your one-sided love are hard to ignore.

1. You're Constantly Second-Guessing Yourself

If you don't get enough reassurance from your partner and constantly wonder if you are pretty enough, or intelligent enough, or funny enough, and always trying to live up to your partner's expectations, then you're definitely in a one-sided relationship. You tend to focus all of your energy and attention on being liked instead of being your true self and nurtured by your partner. It would be best if you always were your authentic self so the people who genuinely deserve you can get attracted to you and get relationships that match the true you.

2. You Apologize More Than Needed

Everyone makes mistakes. We are not some divine creatures who are all perfect and have no flaws. Sometimes you're at fault, sometimes your partner is. But if you end up saying sorry every single time, even if you had no idea about the fight, then maybe take a deeper look at your relationship. You may think that you're saving your relationship by doing this, but trust me, this is a very unhealthy sign. Cori Dixon-Fyle, founder and psychotherapist at Thriving Path, says, "Avoiding conflict results in dismissing your feelings." Solving fights should always be a team approach and not just one person's responsibility.

3. You're Always Making Excuses For Your Partner

Playing defense is excellent, but only on a soccer team. Suppose you are doing it constantly for your partner and justifying their behaviors to your circle of friends, family, and work colleagues. In that case, you're overlooking something that they are most likely seeing. If the people in your life are constantly alarming you, then maybe you should focus on your partner and see where the signs are coming from.

4. You Feel Insecure About Your Relationship

If you are never indeed at ease with your partner and often question the status of your relationship, then it's a clear sign that you are in a one-sided relationship. If you focus more on analyzing yourself, becoming more alluring, and choosing words or outfits that will keep your partner desiring you, then it's a major red flag. To feel unsettled and all-consumed in a relationship is not only exhausting, but it's also sustainable. Feeling constantly depleted in your relationship is also a sign that it's one-sided.

5. You're Giving Too Much

Giving too much and expecting just a little can never work in the long run. Suppose you're the only one in the relationship who makes all the plans. Do all the chores, remember all the important dates and events, consider stopping or making your partner realize that they aren't giving much in the relationship. Often when people give, they have some expectations in the back of their mind that the giving will be returned, but things fall apart when the other person never had those intentions. It's normal for a short while for one partner to carry the load more than the other; all relationships go through such stages, but constantly engaging in it is unhealthy.

6. You're Never Sure About How They Are Feeling

You can't read people's minds, nor are the communications transparent; you may end up overthinking their behaviors towards you and may be confused about how they're truly feeling. This uncertainty would cause you to dismiss your feelings in favor of thinking about them. This connection may be filled with guessing and speculations rather than knowing reality and seeing where they genuinely stand.

Conclusion

The best way to fix a one-sided relationship is to step away and focus on your self-worth and self-growth instead of trying to water a dead plant. You must focus on flourishing your own life instead of shifting your all to your partner. Your mental health should be your priority.

Chapter 6:

10 Signs You're Not Ready To Be In A Relationship

Do you feel the societal pressure to date but can't get yourself into it? Or if you have started dating, ever wondered why your dates go well but you never hear from the person again? Or why despite your best efforts, you can't keep a relationship working? But maybe the problem isn't out there but within yourself.

A relationship can either be the most beautiful thing in your life or the worst. It's not always candlelight dinners and a bed of roses. It requires a strong sense of responsibility and commitment to your significant other. You may feel like you're doing your best, but there are a few factors you should consider that might be keeping your relationships at a distance.

1. **You get overly dependent on people.**

Being emotionally dependent on people sometimes is normal as it is in humans' nature to get reassurance every once in a while. But getting utterly relied on a person to make yourself feel better about yourself can get you nowhere. Your emotions shouldn't be driven by what others might feel or think about you, instead solely by how they will affect you. No one can define your self-worth better than yourself. Try to avoid being too clingy and needy and keep a safe distance from the people you love so you might not annoy them.

2. Your insecurities reflect on your behavior.

Whether you have insane trust issues or you feel like you're not good enough, you start showing the signs of your insecurities in your behavior. You start overthinking everything that your partner does; even a slight change in his/her tone is enough to keep yourself wide awake at night. You get incredibly jealous even if your partner does so much as breathe in the direction of someone else. But as they say, that trust is the critical element of a relationship, so why not trust your significant other wholeheartedly and work on yourself to change your pattern of behaviors that may negatively affect your relationship.

3. You can't stop analyzing your past relationship.

This is perhaps the most crucial factor as to why relationships usually don't survive. You're still hung up on your ex and compare everything your new partner does to what your old partner used to do. You spend most of your time clinging to your past, daydreaming, or perhaps imagining the situations where you could've right all the wrongs. It's usually not fair to your new partner. Yes, it's not easy to just forget someone and move on, but don't get into a new relationship until and unless you're revived from the old one. Give yourself as much time as you want to murder those old feelings, and when you're done, get yourself out there and enjoy life.

4. You try to change who they are as a person.

Another reason that you can't get yourself into dating is that you're always looking for someone perfect, or if you've already found someone, you're molding them into someone they're not. You're always looking for someone with specific traits that you've written on your bucket list for a long time. You have created an ideal image about your significant other that your start losing your mind if something even minor deviates from it. But isn't love all about accepting someone with all their flaws and weaknesses? Instead, we should try to better ourselves first.

5. You're afraid of a serious commitment.

Maybe the idea of sharing your life and thoughts with someone scares you. You might think, Isn't it too soon to let someone see all of your goods and bad? You haven't fully experienced your life on your own yet. You want to travel the world or do academically better, or maybe you want to spend some alone time. Giving someone your time and energy and being there for them isn't your cup of tea at the moment. The best you can do is be honest and tell them you're not ready for something serious yet.

6. **You don't love yourself enough and have serious self-doubts about yourself.**

We all go through our cynical phases where we feel like we're not worthy of love. But being in that constant phase might affect you terribly. You can't expect someone to love you if you don't even love yourself. Having self-doubts sometimes is normal too, but getting them to a point where your partner might feel irritated and it starts influencing your relationship isn't healthy. We should accept ourselves for who we are, take constructive criticism, and try to be a better person for what it's worth.

7. **You have your walls built up and are emotionally unavailable.**

You don't consider sharing your feelings and thoughts with people. You try to solve every problem independently and isolate yourself from your loved ones now and then. The moment a minor inconvenience happens, or you're upset about anything, you tend to distance yourself from everyone. You don't care enough about other's problems too but rather run from them. No one wants a partner who distances himself; instead, being vulnerable and weak looks attractive. It gives your significant other the confidence that you're true to them with your emotions.

8. **You have poor communication skills.**

Communication is as vital as any other thing when it comes to relationships. If you tend to keep something that bothers you and not express it, you might find yourself in a never-ending pit of overthinking and imagining the worst-case scenarios. Your partner may feel irritated by your constant behavior changes and not knowing the reasons behind them. Talking and sorting out the things concerning you anchors your relationship well and gives you a boost of confidence.

9. **You think that a relationship is your prescription for boredom and loneliness.**

Another primary reason why relationships don't last long these days is that people want to kill their boredom by acquainting with another person. They're bound to put in extra efforts just for the sake of their relationship working out and them not ending up alone. You're willing to make sacrifices just to make the other person happy. This affects your mental state as you're emotionally drained out and always looking for people to cope with your loneliness. But if you aren't happy single, you won't be as comfortable in a relationship too.

10. **You're incredibly inconsistent with people.**

One day you're making them feel like they're on top of the world, and the next day you're crashing them to the ground. You're confused about your feelings for them and are not treating them properly. You might act like the perfect person they can get your hands on, but another moment you might work like you don't even give two cents about them. This might leave your partner in a state of anxiousness and confusion because you're not fully committing to your feelings for them.

In conclusion, it's completely okay not to be in a relationship and not fall victim to societal norms if you're not ready. We should practice self-love before anything else, try to be at peace with ourselves first so that we might be able to bring peace into our partner's life too. I hope these points bring you a new self-awareness and you focus more on the attitude adjustments that will eventually guide you to a path to be ready.

If you found this video helpful, don't forget to like, subscribe, comment, and share this with someone important to you. I hope you learned something valuable today. Take care, have a good rest, and till the next video ☺

Chapter 7:

10 Signs You're Falling In Love

As our Literature master, Shakespeare, once said, 'A heart to love, and in that heart, courage, to make's love known.'

Ah, love! A four-lettered small word that leaves such a heavy impact on people. Falling in love is nothing short of a beautiful experience, but it can also give you a veritable roller-coaster of emotions. From feeling unsure to terrifying, disgusting, exhilarating, and excited, you might feel it all. If your mobile screen pops up and you're hoping to see their name on the screen, or you're looking for their face in a crowd full of thousands, then you, my child, are doomed! You are well familiar with the feeling of getting butterflies just by hearing their voice, the urge to change your wardrobe completely to impress them, the constant need to be with them all the time. It is known that people who are in love tend to care about the other person's needs as they do their own.

You often go out of their way for their happiness. Whether it's something as small as making their favorite dish or impressing them with some grand gestures, you always try to make them feel content and happy.

If you're in the middle of some casual inquiry into whether you're falling in love, then we are here to help you. Below are some signs for you to discover if it's really just simply a loss of appetite or if you're merely lovesick.

1. You don't hesitate to try new things with them:

One of the factors that you could look into is that you become fearless and more adventurous when you are in love. You don't hang back to step out of your comfort zone and engage in all your partner favors' activities and interests. Suddenly the idea of trying sushi or wearing something bright doesn't seem so crazy. You are willing to be more daring and open to new experiences. You are ready to go on that spontaneous trip with them and make memories, all while being a little scared inside. But isn't love all about trying new things with your partner? The New York Times article in 2008 revealed that people in a relationship who try new hobbies together help keep the spark alive long after the honeymoon phase is over.

2. You're always thinking about them:

When you are in love, you always tend to think about your partner. Rehash your last conversation with them, or simply smiling at something they said, or questions like what they must be doing right now, have they eaten their meal yet, did they go to work on time or were late again, are always on the back of your mind. You are mentally, emotionally, and physically impacted about caring for them. But it isn't overwhelming. Instead, you get a sense of a calm and secure reality that you will constantly crave. When in love, we tend to merge with that person in such a way that they start to dominate our thoughts and we become wholly preoccupied with them.

3. You become anxious and stressed:

According to a psychology study, falling in love could also cause higher levels of cortisol, a stress home, in your body. So the next time you feel jittery or anxious, that person might mean more to you than you think. You might become anxious to dress up nicely to impress them, or if they ask you something, the pressure of answering them intellectually can be expected. But suppose you're feeling overly anxious about your partner, like them not texting you back instantly or thinking they might be cheating on you. In that case, it's an indication of insecure attachment, and you might want to work on yourself to avoid feeling like this.

4. You become inspired and motivated:

A few days ago, you needed the motivation to get out of bed. And now, the future suddenly seems so bright and full of potential. Your partner inspires you to set up new goals, have a positive attitude, and cheer you from behind while you feel full of energy and chase them. When we are in love, a part of our brain, considered the reward system, releases excess dopamine, and we feel invincible, omnipotent, and daring. Your life becomes significantly better when you're around them.

5. You become empathetic towards them:

It's not a secret that you start seeing your partner as an extension of yourself and reciprocate whatever they feel when you fall in love. Suppose they are accepted into their favorite program, or they expect to receive that interview call, or their favorite football team might have lost in the quarters. In that case, you might feel the same excitement, happiness, or distress that your partner does. Becoming empathetic towards your partner means making sacrifices for them, like going to the grocery store because your partner is tired or refueling their tank in the cold so that they don't have to step out. According to an expert, "Your love is growing when you have an increased sense of empathy toward your partner. When they feel sad, you feel sad. When they feel happy, you feel happy. This might mean going out of the way to give them love in the way that they want to receive it, even if it is not the way you would want to receive love."

6. It's just plain easy:

You don't have to put in extra effort, and it doesn't seem to drain your energy. Instead, you feel energized and easy. You can be your complete, authentic self around them. And it always just seems to go with the flow. Even the arguments don't feel much heated as they did in the other relationships. When you're in love, you prioritize your partner over your pride and ego. You don't hesitate to apologize to them and keep your relationship above everything. When you are with your partner, and it doesn't feel like hard work, know that they are the one!

7. You crave their presence:

Some theorists say that we are more drawn to kissing, hugging, and physical touch when we fall in love. Physical closeness releases a burst of the love hormone termed Oxytocin, which helps us feel bonded. Of course, you don't want to come as someone too clingy who is permanently attached to his partner's hip, but knowing where your person is or how their day went is what you should be looking forward to. On the flipside, Corticotrophin is released as part of a stress response when we are away from our partner, which can contribute to anxiety and depression.

8. You feel safe around them:

It takes a lot of courage for people to open up to their partners. If you don't mind being vulnerable around them, or if you've opened up to them about your dark past or addressed your insecurities, and they have listened contently to you and reassured you. You have done vice versa with your partner, then that's just one of the many signs that you both are in love with each other. Long-lasting love gives you a solid ground and a safe space where you can be upset and vulnerable. When we feel an attachment to our partner, our brain releases the hormones vasopressin and Oxytocin, making us feel secure.

9. You want to introduce them to your family and friends:

You just never shut up about your love interest over the family dinner or when hanging out with your friends. They know all about them, from their favorite spot in the city to the color of their eyes, to how much you adore them and want to spend every single minute talking about them. And now all your family members and friends are curious to meet the guy/girl they have been listening about for the past few weeks. You want to introduce them into every aspect of your life and want it to last this time. So, you make perfect arrangements for them to meet your friends and family, and on the other hand, threatens them to behave Infront of him/her.

10. You care about their happiness:

When you put them and their feelings first, that's how you know it's true love. You don't just want happiness for yourself only, but instead wants it in excess measure for your partner. According to marriage researchers at UC Berkeley, " Spouses who love each other stay together longer, be happier, and support each other more effectively than couples who do not love each other compassionately." You want to go out of your way, or do their favorite thing, to see a smile on their face.

Conclusion:

If you relate to the signs above, then you've already been hit by the love cupid. Scientists have discovered that falling in love, is in fact, a real thing. The brain releases Phenylethylamine, a hormone known for creating feelings of infatuation towards your significant other. The mix and match of different hormones released in our body while we are in love are wondrous. If you have gotten lucky and found a special someone for yourself, then cling to them and don't let them go! If you found this video helpful, please like and subscribe to the channel. Also don't forget to share this video with someone who you find might benefit from this topic as well!

Chapter 8:
8 Signs A Girl Likes You

The human mind is considered one of the most complicated organs, and understanding the female mind can be a hell of a task. In 2017, a professor of neurobiology and behaviour, Larry Cahill, Ph.D., issued the differences between a male and a female mind in his research The Journal of neuroscience. He says that although the total brain size of men is more extensive than women, but a woman's hippocampus, critical to learning and memorization, is more significant than a man's and works differently. The two hemispheres of a woman's brain talk to each other more than a man's do.

Women are fascinating, inspiring, and quite complex creatures. And if you're unsure about the signs that a girl might like you, then you're in it for the long run. Mostly, men are expected to make the first move, like approaching a girl, striking up a conversation, or simply asking a girl out on a date. But women play the lead role in deciding whether a man can initiate romantic advances. They initiate the contact by subtly providing cues if the communication is welcome or not.

It's difficult to decipher a woman's behavior, especially if she's giving you mixed signals. But worry not! we're here to help you see the signs clearly of whether a girl likes you or not. So, save yourself some stress, put your decoder ring on, and let's get started.

Here are 8 signs to know if a girl likes you...

1. She makes eye contact and holds it.

While a lot of people shies away when making eye contact, if you see a girl holding it for more than a fraction of a second (3-5 seconds max), then there's a strong possibility that she's into you. Research says that when you see something that your brain likes, it releases oxytocin and dopamine into your system. These hormones make you feel incredibly joyous. Notice her eyes the next time she makes eye contact with you; if her pupils dilate, then she's definitely interested in you.

2. She laughs at all your jokes (even the lame ones).

When a woman notices a man she's interested in, she would smile, laugh, and giggle more often around him. Even if your jokes are terrible (everyone agrees), but this girl would act as if you're the funniest guy she's ever met. If she counterattacks you with the same humorous and playful banter instead of getting offended, then she's really interested in you. Relationship expert Kate Spring says humor is a sure-fire sign of confidence. And confidence sparks something deep inside women that sets off instant attraction.

3. She mirrors your behavior.

A study published in the Personality and Social Psychology Bulletin proved that subtle "behavioral mimicry" indicates that you're attracted to that person. You might notice that she has adopted your slang, the way that you move your hands while making a conversation, or the pace at which you talk. Jane McGonigal, researcher and author of The New York Times bestseller "Reality is Broken", calls mirroring a love detector. She says, "....the more we feel like we really understand somebody, we're really connecting with them, we're really really clicking with them, the more likely we are to mirror what they're doing physically."

4. She makes frequent contact with you.

Instigating conversations can be a lot of hard work for a woman since they expect the opposite gender to start the chit-chat. So, if she's constantly engaging in discussions with you, making efforts by replying to you properly, and getting to know you better, she certainly likes you. Relationship expert Dresean Ryan says, "Believe it or not, something as simple as a good morning text can show someone has deep feelings for you."

5. She touches you.

One of the most obvious signs that she's into you is when she touches you. It could be a light brush of her hand against yours, slapping your shoulder playfully, or touching your leg or hair. If she's initiating the touch and does not creep out by yours, instead she seems comfortable with you, then it's a great sign of her being interested in you. According to behavior analyst Jack Schafer, "women may lightly touch the arm of the person they are talking to. This light touch is not an invitation to a sexual encounter; it merely indicates that she likes you."

6. She gets nervous around you.

If you're around and she seems to become quiet all of a sudden or starts avoiding you, then know that she's nervous and not uninterested. She might start playing with her hair, rubbing her hands, interlacing her fingers, blink frequently, or compress her lips. If you also notice that her breathing has become ragged and fast when you've entered the room, then that's a lucky sign for you.

7. She's always available for you.

Whether you're in a middle of an existential crisis at 3 in the morning or simply want to go for lunch, you text her, and she's at your door the minute after. Even if she's busy, she'll move things around her schedule just to fit you in. You can easily tell by her body language and her behaviors that she loves spending time with you. She's always there for you whenever you need something, going through a bad phase, or enjoying life.

8. Her friends know about you.

Women tell their friends everything. And by everything, I mean every single thing. So, if she's confident enough to introduce you to her friends, then consider yourself lucky. If they tease her when you're around or start praising her more in front of you, then there's definitely more to the matter. The approval of family and friends is the most critical aspect in seeing whether the individual cares enough to see a future with you.

Conclusion:

Figuring out if a woman likes you is a very tricky business. You might get silences or mixed signals in the initial few days. But it would be best if you looked for the social cues that women give off when they're attracted to you. Try your best and do not give up, you'll eventually get her!

PART 2

Chapter 1:

7 Signs You Have Found A Keeper

Are you looking for Mr. or Mrs. Right? Or do you think you have found the right person, but how can you be sure? Sometimes, we meet someone who seems like the person you would want to spend your whole life with, but during those times, someone is in for a quick hookup. The only partners worth keeping are the ones that give you the positive vibes that you need after a dull and tedious day, the ones that make you feel happy, and your relationship doesn't feel boring at all. Here are signs that you have found a keeper.

1. They inspire you to become a better person:

When we meet someone very kind, helpful and overall a friendly person that person usually inspires us to be better and luckily the world is full of friendly people. Is your partner like this too? Is he warm, kind, and helpful? Does he inspire you to become a better version of yourself? Then you know you have found yourself a keeper. You know you have found the right person when your partner works hard, gives you and his family time, and has his life organized.

2. They are always there:

There are times when we all suffer when things get tough to handle. At times like these, a person always needs support and love to get through the hard times. If your partner is there for you even when you can't defend yourself and they cheer you up, you know that this is a keeper. A perfect partner is someone who knows how to make you laugh even when you are crying, your partner will never believe the things people talk about behind your back, and he would never hesitate to lend you a hand when you need some help.

3. They know you more than yourself:

Sometimes it fascinates us how someone can know us more than we know ourselves; it feels perfect when someone knows how or what we are thinking. If your partner knows what you are feeling without telling them, then they are the one. Does your partner know what you are comfortable with? Can they tell when you feel upset? Do they motivate you to do better and ask you to chase after your dreams? If so, then don't waste more time thinking if this is the right person for you because it is.

4. Your interests are common:

Sure, opposites attract, but too many differences are not usually suitable for someone's relationship. It would help if you had a common interest with your partner, like having common beliefs, values, and religious perspectives. When you agree on these things, your bond will become more robust, and you would find it very easy to live with that person.

5. They are honest with you:

Finding an honest person is a tiring thing to do; many people lie more than twice a day, but how can that affect your relationship? The right one may lie about small things that don't matter that much, like whether the color suits you or not; they may say those things to make you feel good about yourself, but lying about other things like financial status, health, or fidelity can be more serious. A true keeper would never keep these things from you, and they would always be honest with you even if the truth upsets you.

6. They don't feel tired of you:

Although everyone needs some space, even from the person they love the most, he will never get tired of you if he is the one. Your partner will never feel bored with you; on the contrary, your partner will never get tired of looking at you, admiring you, being with you, and above all, love you. When a person is so in love with you that they want to spend every second of their life with you, then you know you have found a keeper.

7. You are a part of their dreams:

Can your partner not even imagine your life without you? Has your partner already planned his future, and you are a big part of it? If so, you know that this one's a keeper. You both have reached a point in your lives where even thinking about living without each other sounds absurd, and then you know that you have found a keeper.

Conclusion:

A keeper is someone that loves, cherishes, and cares for you like no one has ever had. Don't worry if you haven't found your keeper, and it is just a matter of time before you do because, for every one of us, there is someone out there.

Chapter 2:
6 Tips To Find The One

Finding someone who matches our criteria can be a difficult task. We always look for a person who is a knight in shining armor. And by time, we make our type. We are finding someone who looks and behaves like our ideal one. We always fantasize about our right one. No matter how hard it may seem to find someone, we should never lose hope. Sharing is always beneficial. And if you trust someone enough to share your life with them, then it's worth the risk to be taken. The person you chose depends upon you only. The advice can only give you an idea, and you have to act on your own.

Now, when looking for someone from scratch can be difficult for many of us. That person can either be the wrong one or the right one. Only time can tell you that. But you both need to grow together to know if you can survive together. And if not, then separation is the only possible way. But if you find the right one, then it will all be good. You have to have faith in yourself. Be your wingman and go after whatever you desire.

1. Be Patient

When looking for someone you want to spend your time with, someone you want to dedicate a part of your life to, you have to devote your time looking for the one. Be patient with everyone you meet so you will get to know them better. They will be more open towards you when you give them time to open. Doing everything fast will leave you confused. Don't only talk with them. Notice their habits, share secrets and trust them. They will be more comfortable around you when they think that you are willing to cooperate.

2. Keep Your Expectations Neutral

When you find someone for you, they can either leave you disappointed or satisfied. That all depends on your expectations. If you wait for prince charming and get a knight, then you will be nothing but uncomfortable with them. Keep them neutral. Try to make sure that you get to know a person before passing your judgment.

3. Introduce Them To Your Friends

The people who love you tend to get along together. The first thing we do after finding a competitor is telling a friend. We usually go for the people our loved one has chosen for us. While finding the one is all you. They can play a part in giving advice, but they can't decide for you. When we see one, we want everyone to get to know them.

4. Don't Be Discouraged

You are 30 and still haven't found anyone worth your time. If so, then don't get discouraged. That love comes to us when we least expect it. You have to keep looking for that one person who will brighten your days and keep you happy. Please don't go looking for it. It will come to you itself and will make you happy.

5. Look Around You

Sometimes our journey of finding the one can be cut short when we see the one by our side—someone who has been our friend or someone who was with us all along. You will feel happier and more comfortable with finding the right person within your friend. It will make things much more manageable. And one day, you will realize that he was the one all this time. Sometimes we can find one in mutual friends. They may be strangers, but you know a little about them already. However, finding the one within your friend can save you a lot of trouble.

6. Keep The Sparks Fresh

Whatever happens, don't let your spark die because it will become the source of your compassion. It will make a path for you to walk on with your ideal one. Keep that passion, that love alive. If there is no spark, then you will live a life without any light. So, make your partner and yourself feel that compassion in your growth.

Conclusion

Finding one can be a difficult job, but once we find them, they can make us the happiest in the world. And if that person is honest with you, then there is nothing more you should need in one. You can always change your partner until you find the one because they are always their ones too. You have to focus on finding your own.

Chapter 3:

6 Ways to Be More Confident In Bed

Confidence is something a lot of people inherit naturally, while others could work on. When you're confident and comfortable in your skin, people assume that you have a reason to be, and then they react and respect you accordingly. You can be confident all you want at work or on dates, but what about being confident in bed? Being confident sexually can be enjoyable for both you and your partner. It isn't just at ease sexual, but also it's comfortable with the way you express and experience your sexuality.

Sexual confidence can be measured by how authentically you can relate intimately either with yourself or your partner and how pure and vulnerable you are in that sexual space where you feel like giving your 100 percent to be yourself and communicate the pleasure you desire. Building your confidence in bed can crucially improve your sex life. Here are some tips on how to be more confident in bed.

1. Do What You're Already Confident In

Even if you are insecure and think you lack sexual skills, there must be at least a tiny thing that you might be good at. Maybe you don't feel confident enough about your kissing skills, but you're a great cuddler, or perhaps you feel shaky about touching and teasing but are good vocally. Focus on what you're good at and polish that skill every time you're in bed with your partner. This will help you boost your confidence and might even convince you to try something new with them.

2. Try Something New

Once you start considering yourself as the master of that one skill you have been practicing, you would end up craving to try new things. Start with the things you're less comfortable with; maybe stepping out of your comfort zone might be enjoyable for you after all. You neither have to perfect the skill nor be a master of it, just trying it out can be fun in itself. It might be helpful to broaden the sexual script so that it doesn't look the same every time and bore your partner, but instead, trying new things can be an excellent adventure for you as well as your partner.

3. Laugh It Off If You Trip Up

You can't be good at everything you try in bed, nor should you be. What matters is how well you keep your attitude, and if you can have fun with it and have a great laugh if things go south, that's an achievement in itself. If you have already built up consistent self-confidence, then you can laugh it out loud on something that you can't get a grip on. After all, there might always be some things you'll be bad at and others in which you'll be a master.

4. Focus On What You Love About Your Body

There are instances where we will be utterly insecure about our bodies and features. There are some physical traits that we don't like but have made peace with, while others that we want but don't appreciate enough. The next time you look in the mirror, focus more on what you like about your face and body, be confident in them, and the things you don't like about yourself will vanish automatically.

5. Wear What Makes You Feel Confident

There is no particular stuff you have to wear or the way you have to look to feel more confident, but if you wear a look that you think looks great, you must go with it. Chances are, you will start feeling better about yourself instantly. If you feel more confident wearing lipstick, then wear it to bed, or if you think sexier wearing a lotion, use it before bed. Do whatever makes you feel like a total hottie.

6. Repeat A Mantra

We have all heard of the phrase "fake it till you make it." So, there's no harm in faking affirmations till you start believing in them. Keep repeating "I'm confident, I've got this" till it gets through. Affirmations increase how positively we feel about ourselves.

Conclusion

The task of becoming confident may seem daunting, but these small sub-tasks are an easy way to start. Another plus point is once you have practiced these techniques in bed, the confidence will spill over into every area of your life.

Chapter 4:

6 Behaviors That Keep You Single

Dating may not be as easy as it is shown in all those romantic Hollywood movies. There is so much more than appearance and stability in dating someone. And when you are old enough to be involved with someone, you sometimes find yourself uninterested. You think about how everyone your age has already started dating while you are back there eating junk and watching Netflix. It might appear to you that being in a relationship is tiresome, and you stop trying for it. Everyone has a different preference when it comes to finding someone for themselves. You tend to look for someone that matches your knight in the shining armor, which makes it hard for you to find someone you need.

Be true to you yourself while finding someone to date. Looking for someone with the expectation that you are rich and handsome would be foolish. It would be best if you worked on yourself more than that. Make yourself ease around with people but no so much that they start to get annoyed. Don't get in your way.

1. **Trust Is Essential**

Trusting each other is an important factor for dating someone. If you don't trust your partner even in the slightest, then nothing will matter. You will constantly doubt each other. Both of you will eventually fall apart if there is no trust. And if you have trust issues, it will be difficult for you to find someone worthy. But, if you trust too quickly, then it's only natural that you will break your bubble of expectations. Be friendly. Try to get to know them properly before making any assumptions about them. You don't want to go around hesitating about everything. Find yourself a reliable partner that trusts you too.

2. Too Many Expectations

Expecting too much from your partner will lead to only one thing. It leads towards Disappointment. It would help if you let them be. Don't expect things to go your way always. Your knight in the shining armor may be a bookworm because people find love in the most unexpected places. It doesn't always mean to keep no expectations at all. To keep the expectations low. You will get surprised constantly when you don't know what's coming your way. Don't let people cloud your judgment, and keep high standards about a relationship. Everyone has their share of ups and downs. Comparison with others will not be suitable for your relationship.

3. Have Self-Confidence

One has to respect itself before anything else can. You have to have self-esteem in you for people to take you seriously. It is true "you can't love someone unless you learn to love yourself first." You tend to feel insecure about yourself. Everything around you seems too perfect for you. And you constantly think that your partner will stop loving you one day. That fear of yours will get you nowhere. Try to give yourself as much care you can. It doesn't hurt to be loved.

4. Don't Overthink

You found a guy, and He seems to be excellent. But you start to overthink it. Eventually, you let go. That is what you shouldn't have done. Just try to go with the flow sometimes. Don't try too hard for it. Go for it the easy way. Overthinking will lead you to make up scenarios that never happened. Just let it be and see where it goes. Be easy so people can approach you. Think, don't overthink.

5. Involving Too Many People

When you initially start dating, you get nervous. People get help from their friends sometimes. But it is not necessary to get every move through them. Involving them in everything will only get your partner get uncomfortable and get you frustrated. People tend to give a lot of opinions of their own. You will get confused. So, it is good to keep these things to yourself. Be mindful in giving them a brief report from time to time. However, keep them at a reasonable distance.

6. Giving Up Too Quickly

If it doesn't work initially, it does not mean that it will never work. Patience is an essential element when it comes to dating anyone. Don't give up too quickly. Try to make it work until it's clear that it won't. Give it your all. Compromise on things you can. Because if both of you are not willing to compromise, it will not work between you both. It will work out in the end if it's meant to be. Don't push it if it's not working too.

Conclusion

It is hard; it keeps going at a pace. But all you must need is that spark that keeps it alive. Make it work until it doesn't. Go for it all. Make commitments only when you are sure about your choice. And be true to your words. Who wants to be single forever?

Chapter 5:

5 Signs Someone Only Likes You As A Friend

There's nothing like the feeling of getting friend-zoned by a guy/girl you so desperately wanted to be with. When theoretical physicists started talking about black holes, they were probably referring to the friend zone. You find yourself drooling and crushing hard over them, only to find out that they have never reciprocated those feelings. Spotting the signs that they just want to be friends with you and nothing more is always disappointing. But the sooner you see them, the easier it will be for you to move on.

Sure, it might be a little complex for you at first, as some people tend to be very poor in communicating and can give mixed signals, which might make you confused. It could lead to a bunch of misunderstandings between you two and may also cause you to daydream about them when there isn't anything for you. Here are some subtle signs that they only like you as a friend.

They Never Get Jealous

Overly jealous people can be considered toxic ones, and jealousy isn't always a good thing. But sometimes, in small amounts, it might show that one person does care enough about the other to want them all to themselves. If the person you like never gets jealous when you're flirting with other people, or when others are showing their interest in you, then it means they don't care about your love life and sees you only as a friend who's having fun. On the contrary, if they show some emotion or are affected by you flirting with others, it might mean they're interested in you.

They Are Always Trying To Set You Up With Their Friends

If you're romantically interested in someone, then it's not a great sign if they're your matchmaker all the time. Relationships might start like this only in the movies, while the reality is different. It's improbable that someone would set up a person they like with their friend or their acquaintance. If they're constantly on your nerve asking you to date people or are being your wing person, then it's a sign they consider you only as a friend.

There's No Flirting From Their

If two people are really into each other and spend most of their time together, then it's nearly impossible for them not to flirt, even if it's a little bit. It's always in their subconscious mind to praise and appreciate someone they like. While some people aren't the flirty type, and some are just straight-up awkward or shy, we can always filter out if they're petrified or just downright ignoring us. If they don't flirt with you ever, like in any way, or if your flirty remarks make them uncomfortable and they reject your attempts straight away, then it could mean that they're not interested in you.

They Discuss Their Love Life With You

Most of the time, people wouldn't gush about their romantic lives in front of you if they seem interested in you. It would simply send out the signal that they aren't available to you. They might talk about their ex-lovers to try to make you jealous or talk about people who are into them to try to impress you, but that's an entirely different kettle of fish. While it can be hard to tell the difference, see if he genuinely seeks your love advice or seems overly interested in someone else. That would mean he likes someone else and not you.

They Rarely Text You Or Asks About You

When someone likes you, they tend to find excuses to text you and talk to you all the time. They might start by asking silly questions that they already knew the answer to, or may indulge in deep conversations with you, or direct the subject elsewhere so that they have a chance to talk to you. They might even ask your friends or friends about you and try to find you when you're not around. On the contrary, if they hardly text you or call you or even don't try to communicate with you, then it's a clear sign that they might not be interested in you.

Conclusion

You should try and be clear about your feelings and ask them to do the same since day one, as it could save both of you from confusion and getting mixed signals and fantasizing about something that doesn't even exist in the first place. You cannot make someone love you, no matter how much you wish you could.

Chapter 6:

5 Ways To Reject Someone Nicely

Rejecting someone can be pretty hard as we never want that to happen to us as well. But leading onto something that you don't wish to will end up getting you both frustrated and confused. So, it is better to be true to yourself and the other person who feels something for you. That one-sided feeling has to come to a stop at some point, and only you can stop that. You don't need to blame yourself, but an apology would be an excellent way to reject someone. It is, no doubt, the most challenging part of dating.

Try to inform them as soon as possible, that way you will not be wasting any of their time. It can be uncomfortable and awkward to you and them, but it is necessary to do it. And we need to be as gentle and kind as possible while rejecting someone. It can be as hard as getting rejected yourself. It would be best if you picture yourself in their place. It would help if you treated them the way exactly as you want to be treated while getting rejected by someone.

1.Be Honest To Them

When you are rejecting someone, you need to avoid small talks as much as possible. It will only waste your time as well as yours. Be as honest as possible for yourself. It would be best if you told them all the valid reasons for their failure. Keep calm the whole time. Try to be straightforward with the person in front of you. There is no point in dragging things out if the income will be the same in the end. Make sure you try not to hurt them and disappoint them. And after all this, you both have your journey to continue.

2. Choose Your Wording Carefully

You both might go your ways after the rejection, but the words you said will stay with them forever. You need to choose your wording very carefully and make sure it sounds right when spoken. The person in front of you deserves an excellent explanation with a few words of encouragement for him to move on from this rejection. Make sure you choose each word respectfully. Appreciate them for confronting you too. Don't sound too sorry for them. And be very clear on what you have to deliver.

3. Do It In Person

The worst rejection you can give anyone is through a message or a phone. Try to go yourself to reject someone. If you are unable to reach the person for talking for any reason, you have to make sure that you keep the conversation on the phone as authentic as possible. Try to go yourself to give them support. Show them that it is hard for you both to sit there. Its common courtesy to make the other person think that this conversation is vital for you. Show up on time and make sure you deliver your message fully.

4. Don't Give False Hope

If you are not interested in someone, a clear, blunt "no" will do. Don't go by the fear of breaking a heart. You will give that person false hope about dating, and you both will end up unhappy about it. It will waste a lot of your time and theirs. They will move on more quickly if you let them go early. You cannot force the feeling into you. And the other person would be thankful too for your honesty which saved you both from something that was never meant to happen. Just let them be and let them recover from you on their own. That will be the best you could do for them.

5. Don't Blame Them

It would help if you accepted the fact that you are going to hurt them no matter what. And the truth is it was never their fault, to begin with. We cannot choose whom we like in our life. When reasoning, give a lot of "I" statements. Don't point out their issues and faults, and it will only make them hurt more. It is always easier to use the "It's not you, it me "approach with the person you are rejecting. They have to bear with the bad news on their own.

Conclusion

We all want that spark in a relationship, and the lack of it can be equally disappointing to you. But if the other person feels that spark, then you have to light it out quickly. They should move on with someone new in their life and you with someone who can give you that same spark you were craving.

Chapter 7:
6 Signs You Have Found A Real Friend

Life seems easy when we have someone by our side. Everyone makes at least one friend in their life as if it comes naturally. That one person who we can rely on in difficult times. That one person who cares for us when we forget to care for ourselves. Friends are family that we get to choose ourselves. So, we have to decide that person exceptionally carefully. Friends are people who know who you are. You can share both joy and sadness with them without hesitating.

Friends have a significant impact on our lives. They can change us completely and help us shape ourselves into someone better. However, there might be some forgery in your way. Some people consider themselves as your friend, but we fail to notice that it is otherwise. So, it is imperative to choose a friend carefully, while an essential fraction is dependent on our friendship with someone. A good friend is the one whom you can count on to hold you when you require one. A friend is someone who becomes selfless when it comes to us. They always stay by your side as it said, "friends till the end."

1. You Can Be Yourself Around Them

No matter how you behave in front of your family or co-workers, you can always act like yourself in front of your friend. When they give you a sense of comfort, you automatically become yourself. That is the reason you never get tired of a friend. Because who gets tired of being who they are. A friend is a person who accepts us with all our flaws and stays by us even in our worst phase. They find beauty in your imperfections. That type of friend becomes necessary to keep around.

2. A Support For Good And Bad Times

We all are aware that support is what we want in our time of need. To share our difficult times and to share our good news with someone. A friend listens. They listen to whatever you want to ramble to them without complaining. They understand you and try to give to advice as well as possible. They are an excellent shoulder to cry on. They feel joy in your happiness. They feel sadness in your loss. Friends are people who love us, and thus, we give them ours in return.

3. You Trust Each Other

Trust is an essential foundation in any friendship. Otherwise, you are meant to fall apart. It would help if you grew that trust slowly. When you are loyal to each other, then there is nothing that comes between you two. You need to develop that trust slowly. When you are dedicated to each other, then there is nothing that comes between you two. Honesty is a must when it comes to building your trust with each other. If even one of you is lying about anything, then that friendship fails. Even if they didn't keep their promise, you can't trust them.

4. They Hype You Up

They won't fall back on complimenting you when you look your best. But a friend won't hesitate to confront you if you don't look good. That is what we like about them, and they won't make you look bad in front of others. They will make sure you know you are worth it. They will make you work for what you deserve. Friends will always try to hype you up and will accolade you. They know what you like and don't, so they shape you like you want to be shaped.

5.You Share Almost Everything

Two friends are always together in spirits. When something noteworthy happens in your life, you always feel the need to share it with someone. That someone will probably be a friend. You tend to share every little detail of any event of your life with them comfortably. They listen to you. And sometimes, they need to be listened to. That's where you come. You listen to them. Even the most intimate secrets are told sometimes. This exchanging of secrets can only be done when you feel safe sharing them with a person. A friend buries your secrets within themselves.

6. Good Memories

Even the most boring party can take a 360 degree turn when you are with your friend. Times like these call for good memories. It would help if you shared loads of good memories. Even when time passes by, a bad day can make an excellent future memory.

Conclusion

It takes a lot of time, care and love to form a strong bond of friendship. We have to give it our best to keep that bond in good condition. Friends are precious to us, and we should make them feel likewise. And with the right person, friendship can last a lifetime.

Chapter 8:
7 Tips To Get Over Your Ex

7 Tips To Get Over Your Ex

When you get together with someone, it feels like that relationship will never come to an end, but sometimes things just do not work out the way we wanted them to. Break-ups and ending all contact is probably one of the hardest things to do. Sometimes, you start obsessing over them, over the life they might be leading without you. But one thing a person should remember after a bad break-up is that you weren't born with that person; you have lived without them and can do the same again; it just needs a bit of work and time. Here are several ways to get over your ex.

1. Social Media Detox

The most common way of communication is now social media, but we all know its disadvantages. It has made it hard for people to move on; seeing your ex again and again in pictures on social media may provoke some unwanted feelings. So the best way to not feel that way is to get off of social media for a while or unfollow your ex; commit yourself not to check their page or the page where there is a chance you might see them. You just need to gather some willpower and try not to stalk them, which will quickly help you move on.

2. Let Go Of The Memories

When you first start dating someone, it feels right and like you are living in a fantasy. The beginning of a relationship brings many expectations along with it; there are things you expect from your partner and something that your partner expects from you. But when these expectations are crushed, one may feel hurt. A person starts to miss someone when they remember the great times together, so you need to remember that you broke up for a reason. Try to remember what your ex did or didn't do that lead to this break-up. There is always a reason behind a break-up, so place the causes, and you will find yourself realizing that it ended for a good reason.

3. Get Rid Of The Things That Remind You Of Your Ex

In a relationship, we all receive gifts and heartwarming cards and letters, which may make you feel happy at that time, but after a break-up, these cards and gifts may serve as a reminder of your ex and bring back some unwanted but sweet memories. These precious memories can lead you to believe that you miss them. So as soon as you break up with someone, get rid of their reminders. This can include small gifts, cards, clothing because these can lead to obsession.

4. Love Yourself

Loving yourself sounds like a total cliché, but you can never move on from someone without loving yourself. When someone dumps you, you might feel lowly about yourself, and the self-worth you had in mind may get dropped. As much as it sounds easy, it is not. True happiness and love need to come from within. You need to start appreciating yourself, connect with yourself again, and you will start feeling that you don't want anybody else's love to survive because your own is enough.

5. Visualise Your Future Without Them

In a relationship, people make plans and set goals together. So when you break up, you might feel confused as to what to do next, as all your dreams of the future include them. When trying to move on, remember you had a life before them, a life with goals to be achieved. Visualize your future without them; try to set some goals for yourself. Think about all the things you can do now that you couldn't have done with your ex. Visualizing your future without them will help you accept that this relationship is over. You may have a lot of options now that you no longer feel tied to someone. You can set your priorities again.

6. Don't Contact Your Ex

You can set a few rules for yourself when you break up with someone, and these rules should include a no-contact rule at least until you've moved on. Do not contact your ex until you have moved on and accepted everything. Hearing their voice can bring back a lot of memories that will not let you move on.

7. Move Or Redecorate

If you used to share your living space with your ex, literally everything in your house will remind you of them. Move out if you can, but if moving out is not an option, you can redecorate the home, change the furniture positions, and buy some new accessories for the house. Redecorating the house is an activity that you may feel excited about, buy the things you have always wanted but couldn't because of your ex.

Conclusion

Bad break-ups can mess someone up but fortunately, working on yourself can help you move on, so remember that you are a complete person without them, and you don't need them to live your life.

PART 3

Chapter 1:

6 Signs You May Be Lonely

What is that one emotion that leads us to anxiety, depression, or stress? People often feel this emotion when they have no one around to support them. That is being lonely. What is being lonely? "When one is unable to find life's meaning," or simply put, it is the feeling of isolation. You often find yourself in a corner then outside with friends or family. Sometimes, these emotions are triggered by discouragement by close ones and negativity of life. We try to bear it alone rather than risking the judgment of others. We try to hide it as much as possible. Then, eventually, it becomes a habit. Then even if it's news worth sharing, we keep it to ourselves.

Loneliness can drive a person to harm themselves, either physically or mentally, or both too. It can change our lives drastically. Going out seems to be a burden. It feels tiresome even to move an inch. So, we tend to stay in one place, probably alone. But it doesn't always mean that you are feeling sad. Sometimes you feel happy being alone. It all depends on how you look at things.

1. Feeling Insecure

When we look around us, we see people every day. This type of connection with people can lead to two conclusions. Positive or negative. A positive attitude may lead to appreciation. However, negative emotions will lead to insecurities. This insecurity will lead us to go out as little as possible. And whatever we hate about us, we feel it more prominent. Eventually, we never go out at all. Because of the fear that people might judge us at our worst trait. We think that even our family is against us, which makes it even more difficult.

2. Anger Becomes A Comrade

It becomes hard to express what we feel to others. When we feel like there is no one we can genuinely tell our feeling to, they bottle up. We start to bottle up our emotions to don't get a chance to tell others about them. And those bottle-up emotions turn into anger the most easily. Even the slightest thing could make us aggressive. We get angry over all petty stuff, and gradually, it becomes our release to all the emotion. It becomes easier to show your anger than other emotions.

3. It Starts To Hurt Us Physically

Stress is one of the feelings you get out of being lonely. It is only natural that you stress about everything when you are alone in a situation. Scientifically, it is proven that staying alone most of the time raises our stress hormone, and it becomes a heart problem in the future. Most of us have experienced the tightening of our chest at times. That is when our stress hormone raises it builds up around our heart. It may also result in inflammation and some vascular problems. So, being lonely all the time may be physically harmful to us, and we should take it seriously.

4. Highly Harmful To Mental Health

Mental health is just as important as physical health. We need to focus on both equally. Loneliness can be harmful to our mental health in many ways. It often leads to hallucinations. It causes depression and anxiety. These types of mental occurrences are proven fatal if not dealt with immediately. It also drives us to overthink, which is equally as harmful as others. Isolation keeps your brain in a constant phase of resentment.

5. Lack Of Hope and Self-Compassion

Getting lonely sometimes is okay. It gets serious when you do not want to let go of it. When there is no hope, it feels like there is no reason to return—staying alone forces you into feeling empty and unwanted, thus, losing hope of ever being wanted again. Because discouragement surrounds us, we feel safe staying alone most of the time. We lose all the passion we once had, and it makes us dull. Things that once we loved doing feel like a burden. Gradually, we become addicted.

6. Negativity

Positivity and negativity are two aspects of daily life. And in life, when loneliness is our companion, we choose negativity to go through our day.

Everything seems to be too much work, and everything in life seems dark. Negativity is the only thing we keep because it looks more suitable to lonely people. It causes emotional harm to people and tends to get in the way of an average daily routine. However, the negative side is what we choose every day.

Conclusion

We can feel lonely even after being surrounded by people because it's just something people feel in themselves. They don't realize that there are people who are willing to talk to them. Being lonely can cause one a lot of harm and disrupt all the day's work. But it doesn't always mean that lonely people are unhappy. Loneliness can bring peace too.

Chapter 2:

What To Do When You Are At Different Life Stages In A Relationship

If you've started dating someone a lot older or younger than you and you haven't experienced any bumps along the way, it might be because your relationship is still relatively new.

"The issues begin, I think, to manifest themselves when people start to get into real-life situations. For example, if you don't want kids right away and you're dating someone who never wants them, it might not seem like an issue at the beginning. Still, later on, when you start to feel more ready to start a family, understandably, that tiny little thing can become a really big thing.

Not only that, but some people have had issues dating each other because they were at different stages in their lives. For example, while one might want to go out and dance with friends, the other might have no interest in spending time that way.

There are still ways to make a relationship work if you're at different stages in your life.

That doesn't necessarily mean that the relationship can't work just because you have different interests. For example, a woman said that her husband is ten years younger than her, and they don't have the same taste in music. But they each have friends to talk about those kinds of things, and it works for them.

"If you're dating someone with a big age difference, remember the reasons why you are drawn to that person," "Maybe you are very mature, and individuals your age aren't able to connect with you on a deeper level. Maybe you have a fun, energetic side, and you haven't been able to find a partner your age with similar interests and activities."

We advise that you do some reflection about what you want in the relationship to be clear on that and remind yourself of it when necessary.

Make sure your values, morals, and life goals match up.

"If you want the relationship to be long-term, then make sure that your values, morals, and life goals match.

Ask yourself a few specific questions before diving into something. Things like future goals, where you want to live, if you want a family, if you want religion to be part of your life, and if you see this person fitting in with your family and friends.

It's also important to consider what your relationship will look like down the line. "Big age differences aren't as noticeable when you're both middle-aged, but what happens once one of you is a senior, and the other isn't?" "These are the big picture questions that need to be thought about before you decide to spend your life together."

If you agree with each other on the big things, smaller things like having different tastes in music likely won't be as big of a deal. Just like in any relationship, you don't have to (and won't) agree on everything all the time. Although it might seem like you're farther apart on some topics than you would be if you're closer in age, other factors besides age might play a role in that.

Be prepared for others to comment on your relation.

There's a good chance that people will have opinions about your relationship." They'll ask questions, and they'll make comments that are probably pretty annoying, so be prepared with a response. Depending on who the person is, you might actually feel like you can get into an explanation of the relationship, but other times, it might not feel necessary, so just to be prepared with that,"

Ensure that the relationship's dynamic is equal and that one partner doesn't hold power over the other.

Each partner needs to avoid mothering the other, regardless of who's older or younger in the relationship. It can be difficult for those who take on that role, even among friends, to not act that way with their significant other, but she said that it's important to try to refrain. Sometimes mothering can turn into holding power over your partner, which isn't healthy behavior.

Chapter 3:

Stop Setting Unrealistic

Expectations of Your Partner

Are you wondering how to stop unmet expectations from ruining your relationship? Do you find yourself constantly disappointed with your partner and thinking about ending it?

There are ways to stop unmet expectations from ruining your relationship. Here are a few.

1. Identify Your Own

One way to stop unmet expectations from ruining your relationship is by questioning your own. What do you think you need from your partner? Do you need him to give up his friends and hobbies for you? Do you expect to have sex every night? Do you want her to keep the house spotlessly clean as your mother did? Do you expect him to anticipate your every need?

Expectations like these are exactly the things that can kill a relationship. I would encourage you to think about what you want from your partner so that it's clear in your mind. I also want you to consider if your expectations are reasonable.

If your expectations aren't reasonable, your relationship might be dead upon arrival. If you don't know your expectations, your partner will have a hard time reaching them because you might always be moving the goal post. So, before unmet expectations destroy your relationship, make sure you know what yours are.

2. Set Boundaries

I always encourage new couples to set boundaries in their relationships as soon as possible To understand healthy relationship boundaries, look at the four walls of your house. Those walls are the structure that holds your life together. They hold your food and your bed and your possessions, and it's where you live your life.

Healthy boundaries are the same as those four walls of your house. They are the things that support your relationship as it matures. To have a healthy relationship that can grow and be fruitful, it must have structures and boundaries that support it. Healthy boundaries come in many shapes, sizes, and colors.

A few examples:

- Make sure you stay yourself

- Allow yourselves time apart
- Communication is important
- Mutual respect at all times
- Keep the power dynamic equal
- Making time for both sides of the family
- Respecting others friends and hobbies

Of course, each couple needs to decide what works for them, but every couple must establish some boundaries early and stick to them for the sake of their relationship.

3. Be Truthful

You must discuss this with your partner if your expectations aren't being met. One of the most common complaints that I hear from women is 'he should know what I need. I shouldn't have to tell him.' And this, I am afraid, is mostly impossible. Men would love to anticipate and meet our needs, but many of them just don't always have it in them. This is not some deficiency of character but because men have no idea how women think and why. It's a mystery to them, so expecting them to be able to do so will set you up for disaster.

Chapter 4:

How To Deal With Feeling Anxious In

A Relationship

There are different ways in which relationship anxiety can show up. A lot of people, when they are forming a commitment or when they are in the early stages of their relationship, feel a little insecure now; this is not something we would consider unusual, so if you have doubts or fears, you don't need to worry if they are not affecting you a lot. But sometimes, what happens is that these doubts and anxious thoughts creep into your day-to-day life. We will list some of the signs of relationship anxiety so you can figure them out for yourself, and then we will tell you how to deal with them.

1. Wondering if you matter to your partner
2. Worrying they want to breakup
3. Doubting your partners feeling for you
4. Sabotaging the relationship

These are some of the signs of relationship anxiety; now, it can take time to get to the roots of what is causing this. Right now, we will tell you how you can overcome it; yes, you read that right, you can overcome it no matter how hard it feels like at the moment. However, it will take time and consistent effort. The first thing you should do is manage anxiety early as soon as you see the symptoms because you keep delaying it. It will become a problem for you. What will help you is maintaining your identity. When you and your partner start getting closer, you will shift the key parts of your identity to make room for your partner and the relationship. You need to know that this does not help either of you. You will lose yourself, and your partner will lose the person they fell in love with. Secondly, practice good communication. If there is something specific they are doing that is fueling your anxiety, whether it's not making their bed after they wakeup or spending a lot of time on their phone, talk to them about it and try to be non-accusatory and respective about also use I statement these can be a huge help during such conversations. If you feel like things are getting out of control and you will not handle them on your own, talk to a therapist that will get you some clarity. Because it's a relationship issue, try talking to a therapist that works with couples because that can be particularly helpful for you, so if you both have any underlying needs, the therapist will be able to communicate that in a better way.

Chapter 5:

Feeling Insecure In Your Relationship

No matter how perfect a relationship sounds or seems, there is always something that pushes you off on the opposing side. That is feeling insecure. This feeling of being insecure is what makes us doubt ourselves and our partners. A relationship needs to build around trust and feeling secure in it. When you lack those factors, it's only natural that you might fall now or then; it often happens when you feel like your needs are not getting fulfilled by your partner. You will eventually come to realize that you wanted something else. It also occurs when you keep all the problems to yourself, thus, not trusting each other enough to share. These problems then become your demise, and eventually, you are unable to take them. You realize that going separate ways is the only option when you need a good conversation about your problems and listening to what your partner has to say. Giving them a chance and solving your problems together is how you will strengthen your bond, and that's how you will overcome your fears, as we all know that trust is the foundation of any relationship.

It would be best if you let go of things. When you start a relationship with a person you care about, you learn to leave something behind. You watch movies that they like or eat the food they want. Sacrifice is a common ground you both walk on. You have to learn to go by their choices sometimes. But, the same should be done with you. They should do the same for you, if not more. You both need to make some compensations along the way of your relationship. You have to give each other choices. You have to trust each other enough to know that they might be doing the right thing for you or making the right choice for you.

So, the most common factor is trust. Many relationships have been broken because of a lack of confidence. Trust comes very handily when you need to go through a difficult phase of your life. You need the support of your partner, and you just need them by your side. That means trusting them to stay with you through your worst. Growing together is what you need to fulfill in a relationship. And sometimes, while doing so, we meet disappointment. Lack of trust drives you to get annoyed quickly, and you start to get distant. Growing apart may seem complicated, but you think it's better than stay together. These insecurities are very hard to overcome, and all you would need is time. But, know that it is your mind speaking most of the time. That is why taking a chance is such a considerable risk that we sometimes do not bother with it. We have to game risk to know if there is a spark between you two to keep all the light alive. Or if it is just a dead end.

It would be best if you gave yourself a lecture on positivity now and then. It would help if you got rid of all the evil thoughts that are driving you towards doubt. Gain more confidence in yourself and gain more confidence in your partner. Believe in each other. Try to stay positive in every situation. And believe in the best possible outcome of your situation in your relationship. Surround yourself with good thoughts and feelings. Always motivate your partner in the best way possible and think of them as your equal. Share everything, good or bad, with them. You will see getting rid of your insecurities slowly by taking these small measures towards your relationship.

You just need to overcome your differences by talking and listening. Both of you need a little break now and then. You need to give them space often, but not such that they start to believe you are ignoring them. You need to shower your attention and make sure that this whole relationship works out in your favor. Don't get jealous of their interaction with another gender, but trust them to be loyal to you. Give them love and receive love from them. Insecurities are often built on false rumors or accusations. It would help if you stopped a little to process every time. And just know that in this case, your partner's words matter greatly. Make it work out, and try to feel as secure as possible with them around you.

Chapter 6:
10 Ways Men Fall In Love

Genuine and true Love is so rare that when you encounter it in any form, it's a beautiful thing to be utterly cherished in whatever form it takes. But how does one get this genuine and true Love? Almost every romantic movie, we have seen that a guy meets a girl and, sure enough, falls head over heels for her. But translating that into the real world can be quite a task. The science of attraction works wonders for us. Sometimes we are instantly drawn to some people. On the other hand, we couldn't care less for others. And quite a few times, things flow naturally in our direction, making it all feel surreal and causing butterflies.

A famous psychologist once said: "Love is about an expansion of the self whereby another person's interests, values, social network, and finances become part of your life just as you share your resources with them."

A human mind is, nonetheless, a very complex organ. It can either makes you feel like you're on top of the world with its positive attitude or under it with its negative one. And a male mind, perhaps, seems always like a mystery to us. But it's not such rocket science that we can't get our hands on it. If you're developing feelings for someone and need a bit of guidance to get the man of your dreams to notice you and care about you, then you've just come to the right place!

Here are some ways about what a man needs to fall in Love.

1. Always Be Yourself:

Keeping a façade of fake personality and pretending to be someone you're not can be a huge turn-off for men. Instead let the guy know the real you. Let them see who you really are and what you really have to offer. You will not only gain respect from them, but you wouldn't have to keep hiding behind a mask. If you're pretending to be someone else, that only suggests that you're not comfortable with yourself. And many guys will realize this shortcoming and quickly become disinterested. You don't have to dumb down your intellect or put a damper on your exuberant personality. Men like women who are completely honest with them from the start. Who shows them their vulnerable side as well as their opinionated and intelligent one. You're in no need to pretend that your IQ isn't off the charts. Be your genuine, miserable, confident, and independent self always. That way, he will know exactly what he's getting into.

2. Make him feel accepted and appreciated:

From a simple thank you text to calling him and asking him about his day, making small gestures for him, and complimenting and praising him, a man needs it all. Men don't always show it, but they are loved to be told that they look good, they're doing a good job, or how intellectual they are. Sometimes men are confused about where women may stand, and they want to see that he's being supported beyond any superficial matter.

When men share glimpses of their inner self with you and put themselves in a vulnerable position, which men rarely do, this is when it's crucial to make him feel rest assured that he will be accepted and appreciated. If women make men feel lifted high and admired, then it's pure magic for them. His heart will make such a deep connection with you that it can only be amplified from thereon.

3. Listen! Don't just talk:

You would see a lot of men complain that they are not heard enough. And quite frankly, it is true. It's essential to establish a mutual balance in the conversation. Women shouldn't make it all about themselves. They need to let the men speak and hear them attentively, and respond accordingly. Ask him questions about his life and his passion, his likes and dislikes. That way, he'll know that you are genuinely interested in him. Men have a lot to say when you show that you can listen. They'll be more inclined to say the things that matter.

4. Laugh out loud with him:

Men tend to make the women of their liking laugh a lot. When you're laughing, you're setting off chemicals in a guy's brain to feel good. Make him feel like he has a great sense of humor, and he's making you happy with his silly and jolly mannerism. Similarly, men are attracted to women who have a spirit that can make them feel good. Tell him enjoyable stories, roast people with him, jump in on his jokes and laugh wholeheartedly with him. He will become attracted to you.

5. Look your best:

You don't have to shred a few pounds, or get clear, glowing skin, or change your hairstyle to impress the men of your liking. You have to be confident enough in your skin! Men love a confident woman who feels secure about herself and her appearance. You don't even have to wear body-hugging clothes or tight jeans to make him drool over you (Of course, you can wear them if you want). But a simple pair of jeans and a t-shirt can go a long way too. Just remember to clean yourself up nice, put on nice simple clothes, wear that unique perfume, style up your hair a bit, and voila! You're good to go.

6. Be trustworthy:

Another reason that men instantly attract you is when they have the surety that they can trust you with anything and everything. According to love and marriage experts "Trust is not something all loving relationships start with, but successful marriages and relationships thrive on it. Trust is so pervasive that it becomes part of the fabric of these strong relationship." If you want to win a man's heart, reassure him that he can be vulnerable around you and make him feel accepted and secure.

7. Don't try to change him:

"He's completely right for me... if only he didn't dress up like that or snore during his sleep."

Sure we might have a few things on our list about how our partner should be, but that doesn't mean we should forcibly try to change their habits. He might have a few annoying habits that will get on your nerves now and then, but that shouldn't be a dealbreaker for you. Instead, we should accept him with all his wits and flaws. You shouldn't just tolerate his little quirks but rather try to admire them too. If something about him is bothering you, try talking to him politely about it. And he might consider changing it for you!

8. Have intellectual conversations with him:

There's nothing that a man finds sexier than women with opinion and intellect. Get his views on a news article, engage him in a heated debate about controversial topics, put your views out the front; even if they clash with his, especially if they conflict with his, he'd be more interested and intrigued about knowing your stance. Show your future partner that you can carry on an intelligent conversation with him anytime he likes.

9. Be patient:

I can't stress enough that patience is perhaps the most vital key to getting a guy to fall for you. It would be best if you gave him time to analyze and process his feelings for you. If you tend to rush him on the subject, you might end up disappointed. Even if you do lose your cool, don't let him know it. Just be patient and consistent, and don't come off as too clingy or needy. If you appear too desperate, it's going to turn him off of the relationship entirely.

10. **Let him know you're thinking of him:**

In the early days of dating, you might be hesitant to tell him that you're thinking of him. You love it when he texts you randomly, saying he's thinking about you, so why not reciprocate it? Invest your time, energy, and efforts in him. Leave him short, sweet notes, or text him in the middle of the day saying that he is on your mind or sending him a greeting card with a cute personal message. Don't overdo it by reminding him constantly if he does not respond. None of these screams' overboard' and are guaranteed to make him smile.

Conclusion:

I hope this article deconstructed and gave you some insights into what makes a man fall for a woman. As the saying goes, 'Men are from mars and women are from Venus and Venus is great, but surely, we need to know about the inner workings of mars too.' Just keep the above tips in mind, be consistent and commit to him considerably, and you're good to go! If you found this video helpful, don't forget to like, subscribe, comment, and share this with someone important to you. I hope you learned something valuable today. Take care, have a good rest, and till the next video ☺

Chapter 7:
10 Signs Your Crush Likes You

The weak knees you get when you see them, the fantastic smell of their cologne that you can't get enough of, the skipping of your heartbeat when you see their smile or hear their laughter, your face lighting up when you see their pictures. Yeah yeah, we know that feeling very well; YOU'VE GOT A CRUSH! It happens to almost all of us. Maybe there's a co-worker who caught your eye or a classmate that you exchange glances. Or perhaps it could be a total stranger that you have just met and pretty soon started liking them.

You keep thinking about them and their dreamy eyes, their pleasant bright smile, their oh so perfectly structured face, and their lips that are so... but wait! Aren't we getting too much ahead of ourselves?

Maybe, just maybe, they've shown some signs too. They say a crush is called so because they leave you feeling crushed if they don't reciprocate your feelings. But if you've wished upon your lucky star and maybe this time, your star took pity on you and have answered your prayer, then your case might become different than the one I just mentioned.

Getting suffocating and thought-provoking mixed signals from your crush might drive you crazy. You are always left wondering, hoping if the indicative signs mean anything. That may be your crush likes you back too. If you are plucking the poor petals of your hundredth rose and enchanting, 'He loves me/He loves me not,' then save it for later, pretty please?

We are here for you, and using our expertise, we will help you figure out if you are your crush's crush too.

Here are ten signs (in no particular order) that will help you analyze if your crush likes you back:

1. Their eyes are fixated on you:

They say that the eyes are windows to the soul. A study has found out that people unconsciously fixate their eyes on the things they want the most. People tend to keep eye contact with someone they like, apart from the few shy ones who might not like its intensity; perhaps when you will catch them looking at you, they will look away and blush. But shy or not, you have to notice their pupils. Studies show that an individual's pupil dilates when they see someone they like. They also tend to blink more often while watching their crush. If you feel like you are being stared at by your crush or catches them stealing glances at you, and they smile afterward, then consider yourself lucky. And if he's directly locking eyes while talking to you, then that's just the cherry on top of your sundae!

2. Notice their body language:

It is said that actions speak louder than words. Have you ever noticed how you feel around them? Do you get nervous, hyper, shy, or suddenly quiet? Or most importantly, if your crush feels the exact same emotions around you. If he gets flustered or fidgets a little more than usual, or starts to blush or sweat while talking to you, then maybe it's a sign he likes you back. You should also notice that when your crush is standing with you, his feet must be pointing towards you. Weird right? But hey, I don't make the rules. When we are interested in someone, our body naturally leans towards them to be closer. This is a subconscious action that signifies interest. So, the next time you're having a conversation with your crush, notice if he leans in and sits forward with his arms uncrossed, having constant eye contact and listening to you attentively.

3. They're not afraid to open up to you:

It's normal to develop trust issues considering we suffer from terrible experiences, like heartbreaks and betrayals, in our lives. We might have built a protective wall around ourselves to keep people from hurting us. But when we are around someone we trust, those walls come crumbling down without us even realizing it. Whether it's about them spending their next vacations abroad, or their future college plans, or maybe their deepest darkest secrets, they don't hesitate to talk about all of it to you. Experts say, vulnerability nurtures attraction and develops a sense of trust by fostering deeper feelings of closeness. So, if your crush is vulnerable and weak around you and does not shy pouring out their heart to you, then you must be someone really special to them.

4. They want to know a lot more about you:

From your favorite color to your favorite food, to your favorite book, and even your grandma's birthday! They want to know every single detail about you. They remember the important dates and details of your life, even those that subconsciously slipped out from your tongue. Not only this, they never get tired from hearing about you and asking all about you. They might even watch your favorite tv show or read your favorite book to impress you. They make small gestures from the particulars that you have told them. And they are always looking for more opportunities to get to know you better.

5. **Always willing to help you:**

Men thrive on solving women's problems. I guess it's something biological that men always feel the need to provide for the women he cares about, and vice versa. Whether it's giving her his jacket in the cold or her bringing him warm soup when he's feeling down, it all comes down to how much the individual cares about the other person. Your crush eagerly offers you help with just anything and is always available to lend you a hand whenever you need it. The term 'hero instinct' has been given to men who are always ready to help the women of their liking.

6. **They preen themselves around you:**

As soon as you enter the room, you see them adjust their clothes, sleek back their hair, or touch their face, then know that they are trying to look presentable and impressive in front of you. Preening around the people we like is a subconscious way to advertise our romantic interest. We tend to want to look the best around them. From wearing our best outfits to smelling fresh and pleasant and making efforts to make oneself look attractive.

7. **They become flirty/playful around you:**

Another thing to notice is that if your crush is being flirtatious or funny around you. They might try to get your attention and show affection by being playful in a light-hearted and silly way. They might even call you funny nicknames, tease you, or joke around you. It might also be a sarcastic comment or a light punch on the arm or simply laughing with you on random stuff.

8. Their friends act weird when you're around:

If your crush's friends start acting weird when they see you, the chances are that your crush has already told them about you (which, by the way, is basically guaranteed. I mean, who does not say to their friends about their love interest?). Anyways, look for the signs as to how their friends act when you are near them. Do they say their name out loud? Do they giggle or whisper to each other? Do they give you two a playful smile and leave you two alone? Do they randomly start to tell you great things about your crush? Or maybe, they might even ask point-blank if you like the person!

As for you, play along, and maybe their friends would get some sense into them, and they will finally as you out.

9. They try to be always near you:

Do you ever go to a party, hang out with your group of friends, or go to any gathering for that matter but always end up beside your crush? Or perhaps they're making excuses and efforts to see you more often, like a mistaking call or text that results in them asking you out. This might be another sign that your crush likes you; that is, they are trying to get into your proximity. They will try and make sure to spend as much time as they can with you. Whether it's about trying that new restaurant or studying for the English test together, you will see them hovering around you quite often.

10. Their mood changes when you hang out with someone else:

Suppose you are engaged in a deep, meaningful conversation, walking side by side, or just simply laughing with someone from the opposite sex, and you catch your crush feeling gloomy and staring intensely at you both, or walking out of the room, or even joining you guys. In that case, chances are they might be feeling protective or jealous. They want to get all your attention and not share you with anyone else, which is highly adorable. But beware! There is a difference between being playfully jealous and being full-on psychotic possessiveness, which is a huge red flag, and you should probably then stay away from them.

In the end, it is advisable not to assume anything based on just signs and to gut up and tell them how you feel about them. If they reciprocate your feelings, then good for you. If not, then trust me, it'll not be the end of the world; at least you'll be sure of their feelings towards you. And remember, there's always someone out there who would want to be with you. You'll just have to wait and see where destiny will take you.

If you found this video helpful, don't forget to like, subscribe, comment, and share this with someone important to you. I hope you learned something valuable today. Take care, have a good rest, and till the next video ☺

Chapter 8:
10 Signs You're In A Healthy Relationship

Good relationships are a prime ingredient for a happy life, and a bad one tends to be a miserable experience. We all know there's plenty of toxic relationships out there. We've seen them, and for many of us, we have been in them. According to a survey, a third of women and a quarter of men have experienced abusive relationships on average.

The term "perfect relationship" is nothing more than a myth. You don't just get one served on a plate. According to a therapist, "One thing healthy relationships largely share is adaptability. They adapt to circumstances because we can't escape the fact that we're always changing and going through different phases in life." It's not a secret that we all have our ups and downs and ebbs and flows, from time to time. And this may as well affect our relationship too. But one shouldn't strive for a perfect relationship; instead, endeavour to make the best one can.

Let's get to the heart of the matter: How do you know that you're in a healthy and robust relationship, or better stated: How do you know you're in a relationship that's good for you? These signs of a healthy relationship may be blazingly obvious, but sometimes we need things written in black and white for us to see that we're on the right path.

1. **You both understand the need for personal space:**

Healthy relationships are all about interdependence; that is, you rely on each other for mutual support but still maintain your identity as a unique individual. A famous saying goes, "Stand together, yet not too near together: For the pillars of the temple stand apart, And the oak tree and the cypress grow not in each other's shadow."

You don't wholly depend on your partner and know that you have a social circle outside of the relationship. Although you're always there for each other, you don't cling to your partner for every little need, and you spend your time pursuing your interests and hobbies too. Having your freedom in a relationship means that your partner should support your life outside the relationship and might not feel the need to know or be involved in every part of your life. And that means giving your partner the same freedom and independence. In other words, your relationship is balanced.

2. **You can talk to each other about anything and everything:**

They say that secrecy is the enemy of intimacy. And every healthy relationship is built on a foundation of honesty and trust. If you trust one another, you can be vulnerable and weak in their company because you recognize that instead of judging you, they will hold you and support you through the dark times. You're able to pour your heart out to them, no matter how stupid some things might sound. You don't keep secrets from each other. And when you're apart, you're not worried about them pursuing other people. You know they won't cheat or lie to you. You're safe and comfortable with them, knowing the fact that they won't ever hurt you, both physically or emotionally. You know they have your best interests in mind and respect you enough to encourage you to make your own choices. In conclusion, you respect each other's privacy, and the element of trust between you two comes naturally, and neither of you goes out of your way to work hard to "earn" their faith.

3. **You support and encourage each other's passions and ambitions:**

If your partner expresses his interest to become Batman, then you should assure that you'll hold the cape for him. If it's essential for them to, it should be important to you too, no matter how strange or bizarre their goals may sound. Even if you don't see eye to eye on something or have plans that aren't the same, healthy relationships are built on mutual inspiration and motivation; your partner should encourage you to be your best self, to face complex challenges, and to change the world, all by being there with you, supporting you through it all.

4. **You accept them for who they are:**

One of the most critical factors contributing to a healthy relationship is that you don't try to fix the other person. Love is all about seeing the flaws and blemishes of your partner and accepting them. It is about abiding by the bad habits and mannerisms of your significant other and working around them. It is about recognizing all the fears and insecurities and reassuring and comforting them. We all go through our bad days. We should strive to hold them in their bad days and dance and celebrate with them in their good ones. None of us are perfect; we're made with cracks and smudges, our souls have been shattered, and our skin is patchwork. There's nothing wrong with that. When your partner is broken, Vow to hold him together, and when your time comes, to be broken, beaten, restless, except that he'll keep you too.

5. Playfulness and Light-heartedness:

Healthy relationships are full of laughter and fun. It all comes down to joking and roasting each other playfully and laughing your hearts out. The spontaneity and adventures that you both might bring would eventually spice up your relationship. Sometimes one of you, or both of you, might feel emotionally or physically drained, or the challenges or distress might affect your relationship's tone. But being able to relieve the tension and share lighter moments, even briefly, strengthens your connection even in tough times.

6. Conflict Resolution:

Even in a healthy relationship, you'll have occasions where you might agree to disagree. It's entirely normal for couples to have disagreements and feel frustrated or angry with their partner. But that doesn't mean you should disrespect your partner based on his opinions and thinking. It all comes down to how you choose to address the conflict. You and your partner must talk about your differences politely, honestly, and with respect. Know when you or your partner is wrong, and apologize rightfully for it. You should be open to change too. Your number 9 might look like a number 6 to your partner, but it doesn't mean your partner is wrong. It simply means you both are looking at the same thing from different perspectives. Couples should try to understand each other, make their points apparent, and then sort out whatever's bothering them.

7. You feel at ease talking about your past:

Our past might be filled with our darkest secrets, but it does, in no way, defines us. When you feel free to tell your partner all about your exes, and the time you got depressed, and any failures or rejections that you received in your past, it shows that you trust your partner completely. Everything that has happened to your history has brought you to where you are today and changed you into a completely different person. Your partner should reassure you, and you shouldn't feel the need to hide any details from them. Similarly, you should comfort your partner and give them the same assurance.

8. You share responsibilities:

A relationship should always be based on equality. Putting the same effort into the success of the relationship is vital. Yes, sometimes your partner may do their 80%, and you have to put in your 120% and vice versa, but being on the same page and sharing all the responsibilities are a significant sign of a healthy relationship. One of you might be over-responsible in certain things, and one of you might be under-responsible in certain things, and it could be the other way around too. The over/under responsible dynamic is natural. However, when it becomes unbalanced, it can set off a cycle of anger, guilt, hurt, and resentment. Making sure of your particular dynamic and working on your responsibilities allows you to grow as an individual and a couple and balance things out.

9. Making your partner feel loved:

You value your partner's emotions and make them feel accepted and important. You ask them about their day, tell them about yours, and listen attentively to whatever they have to say. You both spend quality time together and make memories that you know you'll cherish forever. You never hesitate to try new things with them, maybe go to a restaurant you guys never go to before or go on a spontaneous trip to another city or country. It might be a shared hobby, too, like joining a dance class, jogging daily, or sitting over a cup of coffee. You surprise each other with dates and gifts. And even though the gift might not be that expensive, your partner will hold onto it forever.

10. Your relationship has gotten stronger over time:

The ultimate sign that your relationship is sustainable for the long term is that it only grew stronger with time. No matter how many times your partner has pissed you off or annoyed you, you couldn't help but fall in love with them a little more every day. Your relationship has slowly built, developing deeper roots with each passing year. The great David Foster Wallace once said, "The essential kind of freedom involves attention and awareness and discipline, and being able to care about other people truly and to sacrifice for them over and over in myriad petty, unsexy ways every day."

In conclusion, if you relate to the signs above, consider yourself lucky and cling to your partner for as long as your destiny would allow.

If you found this video helpful, don't forget to like, subscribe, comment, and share this with someone important to you. I hope you learned something valuable today. Take care, have a good rest, and till the next video ☺

Chapter 9:
10 Signs You're Dating a Sociopath

Opening

Before discussing the signs that you're dating a Sociopath or not let's first understand the term sociopath. It'll make things even more digestible for you.

Currently, around 1 % of the US population is suffering from the personality disorders of Sociopathy. A sociopath disregards people, society, and important societal rules around them. They are extremely self-assured and think about being more talented and better looking than others. Think about Hannibal Lecter, Joker, Patrick Bateman, John Doe, the Buffalo Bill, and many others on the list. Are you a true devotee of Hollywood? Then visualize Charles Manson, Ted Bundy, and Jeffrey Dahmer in your mind. Yes, these are the most precise and realistic character roles of Sociopaths.

According to Dr. Scott A. Bond, Sociopathy is a learned behavior that is often the result of some form of childhood trauma.

Main

In today's video, we will be taking a closer look at the central signs to spot a sociopath so that you can make an informed decision on whether to leave the relationship or to stick it out despite knowing the risks.

1. They get Jealous

Mostly sociopaths get jealous of their partner and blame them for everything. You might find yourself defending against the continuous false accusations of your partner. They would never encourage you to pursue your dreams or achieve anything because of their never-ending jealousy.

2. They Lie about Everything

Lying is never okay under any circumstances; however, Sociopaths lie with every breath. They do it on a regular basis and without any regrets. They find themselves smart doing this because they figure that you might not even know. While trust should be the foundation of any relationship, Sociopaths seemingly lie to their partner with perfection and they are good at planning and telling a foolproof lie which can be difficult to even guess.

3. They are always Arrogant

They constantly consider that they are better than other people are. They are constant swaggers and like boasting about their running speed, nice clothes, or shoes. This attitude in the relationship could be extremely negative, abusive, and uncomfortable. You need to watch out if your partner is always invalidating you and bragging about their capabilities.

There is a possibility that they feel superior in every way and there is no one else that can match the same skill-set they own. If you tell them about their mistakes they will be annoyed and their arrogance in such situations will touch the skies. They might even feel portray that you have hurt their self-respect.

4. They don't think about Consequences

It is often exciting for people to engage in impulsive behavior sometimes, but sociopaths tend to participate in impulsive activities regularly. Apart from being dangerous, it can result in dealing with adverse financial consequences. The same goes in the decision-making process of a relationship. If your partner does not think about the negative consequences of their decision, then you might be dating a sociopath.

5. They don't want to Change

While most people learn from the mistakes and consequences of their poor actions, sociopaths don't pay attention to any of this. These people show zero desire to learn from their mistakes and bring positive change in their attitudes. Their consistently disregarding attitude will make it extremely challenging. Watch out for this sign.

6. They do not tag along with Rules

You may think that it can be exciting to break some rules in the beginning with your date, but if it is a regular occurrence, there may be something wrong there especially if it is an act that concerns criminal behavior. Be mindful that this can ruin your present and future. Watch out if your partner engages in reckless behaviors that are out of the norm and don't hesitate to bring it up with your closest friends and family if you find something amiss.

7. They do not Care

Yes, it is normal to have some days off, but you need to watch out if your partner never cares about anything. A healthy relationship is based upon mutual give and take. If your partner never empathizes with you, then the possibility is that you are in a relationship with someone who might only care about themselves. Since mutual care and kindness are the essences of a healthy relationship, these warning signs should ring some alarm bells for you that you may want to consider walking away from this relationship.

8. They are the Loners

Their antisocial personality makes it extremely difficult to make or maintain a close relationship with others. A sociopath shows extremely antisocial behavior with others and does not seem to have any desire to make any friends.

9. They Relentlessly Ruin Things

A sociopath prioritizes his or her needs over their partner and continuously looks for excitement above all else. They ruin everything with no one left to clean up the mess. If you are regularly facing financial crises left behind by your partner, then you might be dating a sociopath.

10. They have Impulsive Mood Swings

A characteristic trait of a sociopath is that they tend to have unstable or unexpected mood swings, expressing abrupt temperamental changes when things are not going their way. If you said something unexpected and your partner responds with controlling and manipulative behaviors, be careful as this could be another tell-tale sign.

Closing

If any of the above points rang any alarm bells in you, it is time to start paying close attention to these details. Start asking yourself the right questions. While you may have the inclination to give your partner the benefit of the doubt, never become too complacent and assume that you need to stay with someone who doesn't treat you like you rightfully deserve. If you believe that your partner is a sociopath, seek help, talk to a counsellor, your family member, or your close friends. They might be able to paint a clearer picture for you to make an informed decision on the next best move for you.

So, that's it for today's video. Did we miss out on any elements of a sociopath? Let us know in the comments section below. Do not forget to subscribe to our channel, like, and share this video.

Thank you!

Chapter 10:

8 Signs You Have Found Your

Soulmate

"People think a soulmate is your perfect fit, and that's what everyone wants. But a true soulmate is a mirror, the person who shows you everything that is holding you back, the person who brings you to your attention so you can change your life." - Elizabeth Gilbert.

Legends say that even before you were born, the name of your spiritual half was determined. The two souls roam around the world to find their significant other. Whenever they find one another, they will unite, and their spirits would become one. But finding our long-lost soulmate isn't as easy as we think it is. Out of 7 billion people, it could take some time to find out our perfect match. However, when we meet them, we'll click with them instantly and just know in our hearts that they are made for us. A soulmate is someone you keep coming back to, no matter the struggles, challenges, obstacles, downfalls, or any of the circumstances. Everything would feel perfect with them. But how do you know if someone is your soulmate? You needn't worry! We have compiled for you below the signs that you may have found your soulmate.

1. **They would bring the best in you:**

Have your friends called you boring or a party pooper since you have entered adult life? Of course, you blame it all on the fact that you have grown up now and have responsibilities. But there's this one person who tends to bring out the fun and sassy side of yours. You feel so comfortable around them that you're even willing to try new things with them. They make your anxiety and fear go away in the blink of an eye. Be it singing songs loudly in the crowd, trying bungee jumping, or just packing up your bags and moving across the country with them to pursue your goals and dreams, they will strengthen you by supporting your decisions and being there for you.

2. They won't play games with you:

They won't be inconsistent with you, like making you feel special one day and ignoring you completely the next. You won't be questioning his feelings about you or putting yourself in a state of over-thinking. Sure, they won't make grand gestures like showing up at your window holding a guitar at 3 in the morning or putting up a billboard saying how much they love you (although we will happily accept both). Still, they will make you realize your worth in their life by always prioritizing you, making you happy, asking about you throughout the day, and paying close attention to whatever you say.

3. You respect each other's differences:

When starting a new relationship, people tend to avoid or hold back specific thoughts, beliefs, or opinions. This is because, in the game of love, both of the couple's emotions are at stake. They don't speak their mind until and unless they're entirely comfortable with their partner. Your soulmate would always be open to change and respect your opinions and views, even if they disagree. They wouldn't ever implement their beliefs and ideas on you but would instead find comfort in knowing that you both don't have the same set of minds. It's essential to be on the same page with your partner on certain things, like the future, life goals, children, etc., but it's okay to have different moral and political views, as long as you both respect each other and it doesn't hurt the other's sentiments.

4. You forgive each other:

Being soulmates doesn't save you from the wrath of arguments and fights. Every relationship experiences indifference and frustration from time to time. But it is one of the things that makes your bond stronger with your partner. You both would rather sit and try to talk it through or sort it out instead of going to bed angry at each other. And when it comes to forgiving the other, you both would do it in a heartbeat. You wouldn't consider holding the other person guilty and would make unique gestures to try and make it up with them.

5. You give each other space:

Your partner doesn't constantly bug you by texting and calling you every minute. They don't ask you about your whereabouts and don't act overly possessive. And rightly so, you do the same with them. You give each other your space and know that the other person would always be there for you. Even if you have to ask them about some distance, they respect it without complaining. You both trust each other with your whole heart and respect them enough to give them the space they have asked for.

6. You empathize with each other:

If your soulmate tells you about them getting good grades in college, finding their dream job, or getting a promotion, you find yourself being more excited and happier for them than they are. Sometimes, we feel drained out by showing too much empathy to other people and understanding and friendly. But with your soulmate, you don't have to force it out or pretend, and it just comes naturally. Whenever they feel scared or anxious, you're right there with them, protecting them from the world and not leaving their side until you make sure they're okay.

7. You communicate with each other effectively:

They say that communication is essential for any long-lasting relationship. If you aren't communicating well with your partner, you might find yourself in the depths of overthinking the worst-case scenarios. Your partner makes it easy for you to share with them, even if you hadn't done the deed before. You find yourself talking about the tough things, the things that bother you or hurt you, and they comfort and console you reassure you that they will fix it. Similarly, you make sure your partner speaks your mind to you, and you do your best to right your wrongs and clear any of their doubts.

8. You have seen each other's flaws and still loves each other the same:

It isn't easy to accept someone with the habits or traits that you despise. However, you have been your complete and utter authentic version of yourself with them, and they still love you the same. Be it crying loudly while watching an emotional sitcom, binge eating at night, snoring, burping, or just showing them your weak and vulnerable phase when you tend to push everyone away and dress up like a homeless drug addict. They find your quirks cute and accept you with all your imperfections and flaws, and you do the same with them.

Conclusion:

A soulmate is someone who makes you realize your worth and brings out the best in you. They might drive you crazy, ignites your triggers, stirs your passions, but they might also be your most excellent teacher. They would allow you to discover your true self while always being there for you and supporting you all the way.

CPSIA information can be obtained
at www.ICGtesting.com
Printed in the USA
LVHW082222031221
705231LV00009B/245